THE FUNDRAISER'S GUIDE TO SOLICITING GIFTS

Turning Prospects into Donors

Melvin B. Shaw and Pearl D. Shaw, CFRE

The Fundraiser's Guide to Soliciting Gifts

Turning Prospects into Donors

Third Printing – November 2012
Printed in The United States of America
ISBN 978-0-615-60686-6

Dedication

This book is dedicated to the women, men and young people who give their time, talents and resources to organizations and institutions they believe in. We salute your willingness to give and solicit gifts that will make a difference.

We thank Zoe Becker, Bishop Charles Blake, Ruby Bright, Dr. Thomas Crow, Dr. Ned Doffoney, Linda Handy, David Hoard, Lisa Hoffman, Alan Kirschner, Jesse Mason, Rev. Dr. Harold R. Mayberry, Rev. Diana McDaniel, Eleanor Boswell-Raine, Caterina Rando, Lou Rawls, Colonel Shaw, Cherlyn Spencer, Dr. Roosevelt Washington, Vernon Whitmore, our grandparents, parents, brothers, sister, children, grandchildren, cousins and extended family and God for their love and support. We would also thank our clients – thank you for choosing to work with us. Working with you brings us great joy. We believe in your work and seek to support your accomplishments.

Table Of Contents

A Word About Language

This guidebook is created to assist you as you prepare to solicit gifts on behalf of those organizations and institutions you believe in. You may be engaged as a volunteer solicitor, as a member of the development staff, or as the CEO, President or Executive Officer. You may be working with a local non-profit organization, with a national advocacy group, or perhaps you are raising money for a hospital, museum or educational institution. While we recognize that there are differences of scale, governance and capacity, we also know that the fundraising principals and techniques that we share are effective across these differences.

Throughout this book we use the words *organization* and *institution* interchangeably. Sometimes we use both words. Sometimes we use the phrase *Executive Director* and sometimes we use the word *President*. In regards to gender, sometimes we use the word he and other times we use she. Our hope is that, as you read, you will read yourself and your campaign into the words.

We seek to be inclusive, for fundraising – and the non-profit sector in general – is truly dependent upon the goodwill of a cross-section of individuals who believe in the mission and vision of the organizations and institutions they work with.

Thank you for taking the time to help create the world you want to live in!

Introduction

Congratulations! You have been asked to solicit gifts on behalf of an organization or institution you believe in. What an honor! Becoming involved in fundraising will change your life. You will meet wonderful people, increase your strategic thinking, and employ your talents and abilities. As a fundraiser you will become more comfortable talking about money and asking people for money and – most importantly – you will help secure funds needed to make dreams and visions come true.

A common stereotype regarding fundraising is that it involves twisting people's arms and "making" them do something they don't want to do. Some people fear a whispering campaign... "Watch out – here comes Janice and all she wants is your money." *Ah, how far from the truth.*

It is very flattering to be asked to give of your time and money. Many people wait to be approached by the organizations they believe in. They may give for years at the $100 or $500 level, but have the ability and desire to give much more. But they have yet to be personally welcomed into the organization and asked to give their time and money in a more meaningful way.

It is an honor to be asked to give. And **it is an honor to be selected as the person who asks others to give.** When you are involved in fundraising, you represent the best that your institution stands for – its integrity, progress, commitment and leadership. You are chosen for such a role because you are respected by the organization and your peers. Your leadership is visible, and people want to meet with you.

If the organization or institution you are engaged with is working from a fund development plan that honors, recognizes and involves its donors, then you are not begging or passing the hat. **Put those stereotypes out of your mind.** When the fundraising campaign you are involved with is organized and working from a campaign plan you will find that doors open. When the institution is making a difference people want to know how they can get involved and they will want to talk with you.

People really do care about others. They care about their communities and are looking for ways to make a meaningful difference. As a fundraiser you are helping people give to organizations and institutions that improve life. You have access to some of the best people in your community. You have the opportunity to share with them information about how they can contribute to projects they believe in. You become someone people turn to when they want to know how they can get involved or how they can make a difference. Most importantly you communicate with people who have the ability and desire to give but who may not be aware of the needs and impact of your organization.

As a fundraiser you will interact with people who are passionate, committed and active on behalf of the many activities, organizations and institutions that make this world a better place.

Welcome to the world of fundraising.... Your participation will make a difference.

Getting Started –
It's All About Preparation

Asking an individual to make a gift is actually the last step in the solicitation process. And it is the one that takes the least amount of time. Preparing for your solicitation visit is what will consume most of your time and energy. Contrary to popular belief, fundraising is 90% preparation and 10% solicitation.

As a solicitor you need to first make your own gift before you can ask someone else to give. You will also need to learn how to talk about the organization or institution you are raising money for. As a solicitor you will need to "make the case" for why an individual, family, business or organization should give. That means you will need to know the organization's history, its mission, successes, challenge areas and projected growth. You will need to be able to talk numbers and emotions. You will be called upon to explain allocation of current funds, costs associated with growth, and revenue streams. You will also need to talk passionately from a feeling place about what the organization means to you and those served.

You can prepare by studying the campaign's case statement and reviewing annual reports, newsletters and brochures. You will want to talk with those in leadership and you will want to witness the organization's work. All this preparation will make you a better solicitor. Those you want to encourage to give will have questions. When you are prepared and know what you are talking about, you are able to answer questions, and that reflects well on the organization you represent.

Letters Vs. A Personal Visit

When it comes to actually asking for a gift, many people begin to feel uncomfortable. They don't want to "impose." They don't feel comfortable talking about money. You may experience these feelings. You may want to get out of **personally** asking for a gift by suggesting that a letter be sent to those you know.

"I'll send them a letter and they'll give. I think that will be best."

"Add them to the mailing list – I know they will give a gift."

These are tried and tested ways to ensure that prospective donors are engaged at the lowest possible level.

When you want individuals, organizations or businesses to become involved with your organization or institution – and to give in a meaningful manner – they need to be **personally asked** to become engaged. Direct mail – while an important component of a fundraising program – does not yield the results that a personal solicitation does.

Taking the time to ask individuals who have the combined interest and capacity to give is much more effective. Asking people with interest and financial capacity is even more successful when the "right person" makes the ask.

⊃ Special Note

Individuals or businesses who have been giving in response to direct mail requests are often top prospects for a personal solicitation, especially if they have been giving regularly for many years or if they give gifts that are larger than the typical gift in response to a direct mail appeal.

Campaign Information

The following is a list of campaign information pieces that can support your work as a solicitor. Use these materials to increase your knowledge of the institution. Use the materials when you visit with prospective donors. Share them with family and colleagues to increase their awareness of what you are involved in. You never know – they may want to make a gift in your honor when your birthday rolls around!

1. **Case Statement.** A clear, concise and compelling document that outlines the institution's history, vision and successes. The case statement typically highlights campaign goals, how the money will be used and the impact that funds raised will have on the institution's ability to deliver on its mission and manifest its vision. **This is the most important document of the campaign.** It serves as source material for all others.

2. **Campaign Brochure.** This brochure is a "leave behind" – something you leave with your prospective donor after your visit. Eye-catching and easy to read, the brochure provides highlights from the case statement and illustrates the *impact* that giving to the campaign will have. It also includes contact information so the people you solicit can personally contact the institution or visit the website.

3. **Leadership Guide.** This booklet contains everything you need to know to solicit a gift. If your institution doesn't have one to share with you, ask that one be created. A leadership guide includes the case statement, a list of the organization's leadership, successes, bragging rights, frequently asked questions (with answers!), the names of those leading the campaign, how and where to submit pledge forms and checks, a list of naming opportunities, information about sponsorship benefits and more.

4. **DVD.** A short video can make a dramatic impact. Bring a copy to show on your laptop during the meeting or send one in advance.

5. **Gift Impact Overview.** This document shows the impact a gift can make. *Examples:* $500 buys books for a semester. $50 feeds a family for a week.

6. **Naming Opportunity Overview.** A listing of available naming opportunities (and quantities) and gift levels associated with each.

7. **Sponsorship Benefits.** A listing of benefits that accrue to donors and sponsors at specific gift levels.

8. **Giving Form.** Also known as pledge form. This form includes space for donors to indicate if matching gifts are available from their employer, if a gift is in honor of someone, or if it is being made in memory of someone.

9. **Economic Impact Brochure.** While every institution needs to raise money, most also make an economic impact. This brochure communicates the economic impact your institution makes on the community through its payroll, job training, tourist draw, student spending and other methods.

Preparing For Objections

As you prepare for your meeting, consider the possible objections a prospective donor might have to making a gift. **Write them down.**

If you were initially reluctant to make a gift or had questions you needed answered before you were willing to give, include these.

Review the campaign materials and see if the answers to your questions or objections are included. If so, consider highlighting specific text and having it easily available should the issue come up when meeting with a donor. If not, ask these questions of the institution's leadership and ask the development office to write them up and share them with other solicitors as a FAQ (Frequently Asked Questions) document.

Don't be discouraged by objections.

The most important thing is to be prepared to address objections. Sometimes the response to a specific objection is simply, *"I agree. That is a problem."* If the issue is being addressed, share that. *"It's interesting that you bring that up. The board discussed that very issue at their last meeting and agreed to allocate the resources necessary to resolve it."*

Every institution has its fair share of problems and challenges. That doesn't mean that people don't give to them or that they are not worthy investments.

Get Ready!

Before you ask someone to give of their time or money, you need to prepare for "the ask." Follow these steps as you get ready.

1. **Identifying prospective donors.** Those people you want to personally solicit should have an interest in or relationship with your organization combined with the financial capacity to make a meaningful gift.

2. **Rating and ranking prospective donors.** When you ask a person to make a gift to your organization it is best to have a specific figure or "ask amount" in mind. This process of "rating" a prospective donor's giving capacity and interest is important because you don't want to ask for too small a gift or too large a gift.

⊃ Keep in Mind

The ask amount should be relative to the following four factors:

- Level of interest or engagement with organization.

- Individual's or business' financial capacity to make a gift.

- Individual's or business' history of giving to comparable organizations.

- Campaign's financial goal.

This last point is especially important as very few people want to make a disproportionate gift. Campaigns are designed to engage giving by many, not a few. While a family may have given $500,000 to a local museum's $10 million capital campaign that does not mean it is appropriate to ask for $500,000 towards your $1 million annual campaign.

3. **Determining the best solicitor.** Who should ask a prospective donor for a gift? Solicitors should meet the following criteria:

   - Is a peer of the prospective donor.

   - Has made her own gift to the campaign at a level comparable to the amount she will ask the prospective donor for.

   - Is knowledgeable about your goals and objectives.

   - Has a positive relationship with the prospective donor.

4. **Engaging and training solicitors.** Before you solicit a gift, you should be trained in how to solicit. If training isn't offered, ask for it. Solicitation training can be formal or informal. This training helps increase your knowledge of the organization, its history, successes, vision and goals. Role playing should be included where possible to help reduce any "fear of making the ask."

Cultivation

Cultivation is the process of beginning a relationship between the institution and those individuals who you believe may have the interest and financial capacity to make a meaningful gift.

As a solicitor your first task is to develop and cultivate relationships with the individuals you will solicit. Perhaps you already know them. Some may be new to you. While people will be making a gift to your institution, in many cases, they may make their first gift – or continuing ones – because of who asks them.

Because people give to people, you serve as a bridge between people who know and trust you but who may not yet know the institution you believe in. The process of creating that bridge is the cultivation process.

Cultivation should always occur before an individual is asked for a gift. The cultivation process may take a few months or a few years depending upon the individual, your institution and the type of gift you seek to solicit. There is a correlation between the size of a gift and the depth of a relationship between a donor, the solicitor and an institution.

The following is a list of cultivation activities your institution can consider implementing. Think about how you can help with these activities. Where possible extend a personal invitation to the individuals you are cultivating and attend these activities with them. Your involvement, in many instances, is what encourages their involvement.

1. **VIP Tours.** These tours welcome individuals to the facility and introduce them to those in leadership and the work of your institution. They give people the opportunity to see your institution in action and to feel its energy and commitment.

2. **Small House or Office Parties.** Hosted by board members or friends, these parties introduce the leadership and work of your institution in an intimate setting. Be sure to show your short DVD. These typically last no more than a total of 90 minutes.

3. **Personal Invitations.** Invite prospective donors to attend events that are part of the life of your institution. These could be exhibit openings, graduation ceremonies, lectures, press conferences, field trips, concerts, dinners, town hall meetings, receptions or award ceremonies.

4. **Introductory Visits.** A personal visit from the President or CEO says a lot. Introductory visits are an ideal way for prospective donors to get to know your institution's leadership without being asked for a gift. These visits are an ideal time for your president to

ask for guidance in addressing a specific issue. You – or the president – can then stay in contact with your prospective donor regarding its resolution.

5. **Updates and Status Reports.** Prospective donors should be kept informed about the activities, goals and accomplishments of your institution. These written communications are not solicitations – they are information sharing pieces.

Doing Your Homework

It is important that you give consideration to the prospective donor's interests and have an understanding of why she would want to financially support your campaign. The organization's development staff should prepare the following information for each individual you will be approaching. In those cases where you have a stronger relationship with the prospective donor you will be sharing the information with the development staff as they create the profile. The prospective donor profile should include information such as:

1. Prospective donor's relationship with your organization

2. Reason prospective donor would be interested in supporting your organization

3. How the campaign aligns with what you know about the donor's interests and values

4. Individual's history of giving

You will also need to know more basic information such as:

1. Name of prospective donor

2. Title, Job/position/business, primary activity

3. Relationship between yourself and solicitor

4. Date, time and location of visit

Don't forget the basics!

Securing The Meeting

The following is a list of things to consider as you schedule time to meet with prospective donors:

1. Let your prospective donor know that you would like to talk with her about giving to the institution you are involved with.

2. Your prospective donor should always know that she is about to be asked for a gift. *Actual solicitation should not be a surprise.*

3. Meet at the individual's office or home, at your office, or another location that is appropriate for a private and confidential discussion.

   Example: "Hello Dr. Ong, I'm glad you were able to attend our organization's open house last month. I'm calling to see if we can find a time to meet and talk more about the campaign and how you and your business can get involved. Could I come by your office next Thursday afternoon to talk with you about this?"

   Example: "Hello Sonya. I'm hoping you and your husband will have some time for me to visit with you when I am in town next month. I want to talk with you about new developments at our alma mater and explore how you and your family can get involved. "

Setting The Stage

The following is a list of things to consider as you mentally rehearse for your meeting and as you begin the meeting itself. Remember to arrive early and, after initial conversation, make the ask. Do not let too much time lapse before you bring up the subject of giving.

1. Establish a personal connection. Be sure to connect with the person you are meeting with. Inquire after her family members and/or business. Follow up on joint activities or other things you share in common. If a friend of hers has suggested this meeting, be sure to say so. Establish a mutual connection before you begin talking about the fundraising campaign.

2. State the purpose of your visit. Share with your prospective donor why you have asked to visit with him.

    Example. "John, I'm glad you could make time for us to get together today. I want to talk with you about a fundraising campaign for an organization I care deeply about, the Regional Arts Center. I want to share with you their goals and successes and explore how you and your business (or family) can support their work."

Exploration

Share initial information about the institution you are representing. Refer to written information that has been prepared for you by the institution's leadership. Be prepared to talk about the facts, costs and projected outcomes and timelines. And be prepared to talk about the emotional impact of the campaign – why you chose to support this fundraising endeavor as opposed to the many other worthy causes.

Create your own way of talking about the institution and its campaign that draws on available information.

Through conversation explore what your prospective donor knows about the institution and its campaign. As appropriate, ask questions such as the following:

For a college or university:

1. Jesse, have you been back to campus since you graduated? Have you kept up with their new developments?

2. Are you aware of the economic impact that an education from ABC College makes on first generation students and their families?

3. What do you think about this project? What aspects are most important to you?

For a non-profit organization

1. Maria, did you know that Families Helping Families was recognized by the Mayor last year as most effective non-profit organization?

2. What do you think about the way the organization is collaborating with other organizations?

3. Do you think we can implement our new strategic plan? What do you think will come easy and where do you think the challenges will lie?

Presentation

After you have engaged in exploratory conversation you should present information about the campaign, its goals and projected impact. This is the time when you are doing most of the talking. Speak with authority.

1. **Make the case for the organization and its campaign.** Present the aspects and benefits of the organization and its campaign priorities that you feel are most important. Tailor each presentation so that you address the interests and concerns of the person you are speaking with.

2. **Share the materials you have brought.** Bring out the information package you have brought with you and talk about those pieces you think are of most interest to your prospective donor.

3. **Introduce Leadership.** If you have brought the Executive Director or a board member with you, ask him to talk about the organization, its successes and his vision for the future.

4. **State what is needed to bring the Executive Director's vision to fruition.** This is the time to be specific. Talk about the full amount of funds needed and how they will be used. If public funds or a matching grant is available talk about these funding

sources. Do not be afraid that your project is too big or too small. Fully reveal the amount of funds already raised and where you believe the remaining funds will come from.

Example: "This $41 million project requires $4 million in private funds. $32 million has been raised through a public bond measure. We are expecting another $7 million to be allocated through special legislation. Of the $4 million we are raising from private sources $1 million has been donated by College and District employees and leadership. Another $1 million has come from individuals, families and businesses. We are raising the last $2 million and hope that you will join us."

5. **Share the names of donors who have given a gift to the Campaign.** Many people like to know who else is giving to your campaign. Be sure to share the names of people you believe they are aware of. Unless an individual or business has indicated that they are comfortable with others knowing the amount of their gift, use general terms.

Example: "A diverse group of individuals and businesses are supporting this campaign. They include: First Bank, the Community Foundation, Marilyn and Hector Alvarado, and Big Construction, Inc. In fact the Alvardos are very excited about this project and are giving a gift of $50,000 in honor of their parents."

6. **Review benefits available for gifts at different levels.** Come prepared with written information regarding benefits that are available to donors. Sometimes the benefits associated with giving at a certain level can help encourage a prospective donor to increase her gift to take advantage of a naming opportunity or other benefit that has meaning to her. *If you secured a naming opportunity as a result of your giving, please share that information as you are comfortable.*

    Example: "All gifts are recognized with benefits that include naming opportunities, meetings with the organization's leadership, tickets to special events, and a listing on the wall of honor." Provide information on the specific unique benefits associated with your campaign, sharing the campaign information with the prospective donor.

The Ask

Close your presentation with a request for a specific financial gift.

Example: "Elaine, would you support the campaign with a $5,000 gift?"

Pause After Making Your Request.

1. Wait silently and patiently for a response. No matter how tempted you may be, do not jump in to fill the silence. This is the time for you to listen.

2. Once your prospective donor begins talking, don't interrupt. People will provide a lot of information if you give them the time to do so.

When the person says YES

1. Say "Thank you."

2. Let the donor know what their willingness to give means to you.

3. Review campaign benefits and naming opportunities that correspond to the gift amount.

4. Discuss details of how the gift will be made:

   a. Immediate one-time gift?

   b. Amount pledge over time?

   c. Gift of securities or property?

   d. Inclusion of matching gift by employer?

5. Review and complete pledge/giving form with donor. Make sure that names are spelled correctly and that recognition will be given according to the donor's wishes.

If a prospective donor says NO...

Listen to what comes after "no."

1. This may not be the right time for the individual or business to give.

2. The person may have other current giving priorities or constraints. Explore when might be the right time for prospect to give or what might be the right amount.

Example: "George, what would be a good time for you to support this campaign? What would work with your schedule and priorities?" **PAUSE.**

3. If the person you are meeting with does not want to support the Campaign, thank him/her for their consideration and leave the door open for future conversations.

Example: "Elize, I truly appreciate the time you have given me. Thank you for considering this campaign and please let me know if there are other ways, or another time, that you would like to be involved with this."

Objections

The following is a list of objections that could come up. Review these and prepare your responses. Or use these as a starting point to help you identify potential objections you need to be able to address.

1. **I'm really not in a position to make such a gift right now.**

   Potential Response: Do you have an idea when would be a good time for you to give? You could make a pledge now with payments that begin at a time that works for you.

2. **I don't feel that this is a project I want to support at this time.**

   Potential Response: Is there anything specific that you find objectionable? Is there additional information that I could provide you with?

   Or

   I understand and I appreciate the time you have given me. If you do want to get involved in the future please let me know.

3. **I thought they finished that project. Weren't they raising money for that project two years ago?**

Potential Response: We had hoped the project would have been completed by now, but there were cost over-runs and construction challenges that forced us back to the drawing board in the middle of building. We are back on track but the costs have escalated and we are in the process of raising the last $2 million.

4. **I don't support capital projects. I prefer to give to programs and research.**

Potential Response: I understand. In addition to our capital campaign we are also raising funds to support our ongoing programs and research. We would truly appreciate your support in this area.

The Specifics Of The Gift: Questions And Answers

The following are questions that may arise during your conversation. If they don't come up you may want to bring up these issues so the donor and organization achieve maximum benefits.

Can I make a pledge?

Potential Response: Yes. Your gift can be pledged over a three-year period in installments that work best for you. For a pledge to count towards the campaign it must be signed and submitted.

I am thinking I would like to do something to honor my parents - what would it cost to do that?

Potential Response: The Campaign includes a variety of naming opportunities that can be configured to meet your requirements. (Review naming opportunity sheet with donor.)

Can I structure my gift so it comes through my company?

Potential Response: Yes. We can work with you to structure your gift so that it works best for your situation. Company gifts are welcomed and encouraged.

Will a matching gift from my company be credited as part of my gift?

Potential Response: Yes, if that is what you want. If you know your company matches gifts on a 1:1 basis you can pledge $3,000 and fulfill that pledge by giving $1,500 and having your company give the $1,500 matching gift.

Closing The Meeting

Review the following checklist as you prepare to close your meeting:

1. Thank the person you are visiting with for his time.

2. Ask if there is any additional information the donor would like to receive.

3. Make sure the donor has completed the pledge/ giving form. It is best if you take the form with you and return it to the Campaign leadership.

   a. If the donor selected a naming opportunity, is that clearly indicated?

   b. If the gift is in honor or memory of someone, is that clearly indicated? Is an additional acknowledgement address included?

4. Let the donor know you will keep him informed on upcoming events related to the campaign and the institution.

After The Meeting

1. Send a personal thank you note regardless of whether or not the person you visited with made a gift. Use your personal stationary or a campaign note card.

2. Write up notes from meeting and submit them to the campaign leadership. Include the following.

   • Date of visit and who joined you (if anyone)

   • Gift amount asked of donor

   • Solicitation outcome: gift or decline

   • Gift or pledge amount

   • If pledge, terms of pledge

   • Naming opportunity (opportunities) selected by donor

   • Whether or not gift is made in honor of someone or in someone's memory (give name and information for additional acknowledgement)

Acknowledgement and Follow Up

After you inform the campaign leadership of the results of your meeting the organization's staff will ensure that the following occur. If staff doesn't talk with you about these acknowledgement and follow up items, bring up the subject and ask that they keep you informed.

1. Thank you phone call is placed by the President, Executive Director, Campaign Chair, or other leadership.

2. Thank you and acknowledgement letter is prepared and sent that documents amount and terms of gift.

3. Donor receives campaign newsletters, updates and invitations to upcoming campaign events.

4. Pledge reminders are sent as appropriate.

5. Campaign benefits, acknowledgements and naming opportunities are distributed/implemented in accordance with campaign policies and donor's wishes.

6. Donor is invited to participate as a campaign solicitor as appropriate.

The End Is The Beginning

Your solicitation – regardless of outcome – is part of a larger long term relationship. Our hope is that you will continue to stay in contact with those individuals you have solicited and serve as a link between them and your organization. People give to people and you are now that person whom people can turn to for information and updates.

We trust that you have learned to enjoy the process of soliciting on behalf of those organizations and institutions you believe in. If you stayed with the process, we know that you have been successful, that because of your asking people have given. We hope you enjoy the thrill of a successful solicitation. You are bringing new friends and resources to help an organization you believe in. You can make a difference and you are making a difference. You are helping to provide the funds needed to make a difference today and in the future.

We salute your dedication and generosity!

About The Authors

Mel and Pearl Shaw are the principals of Saad & Shaw – Comprehensive Fund Development Services. They provide clients with a unique brand of fundraising that combines marketing, corporate partnerships and the best of business leadership with fundraising fundamentals. The firm is known for designing innovative fundraising programs that increase revenue, strengthen partnerships and provide value to all parties. Core services include campaign research, planning, design and implementation. Clients include colleges and universities, health care institutions, grass roots groups and philanthropy organizations. Principals Mel and Pearl Shaw also write the weekly column FUNdraising Good Times distributed nationally.

Melvin B. Shaw offers more than 30 years experience in fund development and marketing. Formerly the Vice President of Marketing for the United Negro College Fund (UNCF), he created and produced the Lou Rawls Telethon, raising $4 million annually in corporate sponsorships and over $500 million in annual gifts to date. Mel also served as the Executive Director of the Texas Association of Developing Colleges, facilitating joint programs and fundraising.

Prior to forming Saad & Shaw he headed his own firm Shaw & Company, which specialized in capital campaigns, annual giving, development assessments, feasibility studies, board development, campaign designs and planning, and major donors. Mel holds a Bachelor of Science from Lane College in Tennessee; a Masters in Business Education from the University of Memphis; and was a fellow at Harvard University's Institute of Educational Management. In 1991 Mr. Shaw received an honorary Doctor of Humanities degree from Lane College in recognition of his unique brand of fundraising.

Pearl D. Shaw CFRE is a development professional with management experience in the private and non-profit sectors. She has served as Development Director of the Women's Funding Network, an association of 100+ women and girls' foundations; and as a major gifts officer for Mills College. Her private sector experience includes business development and marketing. Prior to forming Saad & Shaw, she headed her own firm, Phrased Write, providing nonprofit organizations with proposal writing, executive coaching, and strategic fund development services including major gifts.

Pearl has written proposals securing millions of dollars for her clients. These include the Omega Boys Club; Regional Technical Training Center; Centro de Servicios; Bay Area Black United Fund; and the American-Arab Anti-Discrimination Committee, San Francisco.

Pearl serves on the marketing committee for the Women's

Foundation for a Greater Memphis. She is a member of the Association of the Fundraising Professionals and a Certified Fund Raising Executive (CFRE). She holds a Bachelor of Arts degree from UC Berkeley, and a Masters in Public Administration from Cal State Hayward.

Related Services Offered by Saad & Shaw

Counsel on Demand^{SM} is a unique and innovative solution to the challenges and opportunities that organizations and institutions face in the areas of fund development and fundraising. It addresses the most frequent concerns we hear as we work with clients across the country.

✓ "We need someone to monitor our fundraising program and keep us focused and on track."

✓ "I need someone to coach me and keep me focused on fundraising."

✓ "I need to learn how to ask for money. It just doesn't come naturally to me."

With Counsel on Demand^{SM} you have access to experts who can help you meet these challenges and manage your fund development resources and staff most effectively. **Counsel on Demand**^{SM} **provides flexible, low-cost fund development coaching and strategy sessions targeted towards Executive Directors and College Presidents.** We also have a program for Development Directors and Vice Presidents of Advancement. With Counsel on Demand you get five hours of on-call expertise each month. Call on Saad & Shaw when you need us and we are there to support you with solutions. For more information contact us directly at (901) 522-8727 or by email at **melandpearl@saadandshaw.com** .